WALKS IN THE

WESTERN DALES

HILLSIDE GUIDES

CIRCULAR WALKS IN THE YORKSHIRE DALES

OTHER TITLES

WALKS
IN THE
WESTERN DALES

by

Paul Hannon

HILLSIDE PUBLICATIONS

HILLSIDE PUBLICATIONS
11 Nessfield Grove
Exley Head
Keighley
West Yorkshire
BD22 6NU

First published 1987
2nd impression 1988

Cover illustration: Ingleborough from Ribblehead
Page 1 : on Smearsett Scar

ISBN   0 9509212 9 7

Printed in Great Britain by
Carnmor Print and Design
95/97 London Road
Preston
Lancashire
PR1 4BA

INTRODUCTION

The area of the Western Dales is based upon two major valleys, the Ribble and the Dee. These rivers rise on neighbouring moorland, yet finish at opposite ends of the National Park. The Ribble leaves at Settle, in the south, while the demise of the Dee is at Sedbergh, in the north. By way of a coincidence these two market towns make the best centres for the area, and they also serve to illustrate the substantial extent of the countryside involved. Although a much wider range of walks could be described, this is mountain territory, and major ascents of the high fells are not within the scope of this guide.

Of the two well-defined areas dealt with, the southern half is the most visited, for not only is it closer to centres of population, but it also contains the famous Three Peaks. Ironically it is these summits that so many come so far to conquer - in this district it can therefore be quieter nearer the valleys! Besides the Ribble there are just two small dales, those of the Twiss and the Doe, which meet at Ingleton. This is limestone country at its most splendid, and these walks take in many of its fascinating features.

Across the heights of Whernside and Blea Moor is the northern half of the guide, linked by the Ingleton-Dent and the Ribblehead-Dent Head roads. In striking contrast this is a region of deep-cut valleys. North of the Dee's Dentdale are Garsdale, the valley of the Clough, and Rawtheydale. All three meet rather tidily in the neighbourhood of Sedbergh. Here too are mountains, and none more attractive than the Howgill Fells, the finest massif in (and out of) the Dales Park. This guide is even divided politically, with the northern dales having left Yorkshire for Cumbria.

Besides the winding roads, there is another method of linking the areas, a majestic, incomparable way known as the Settle-Carlisle railway. Permanently under threat of closure, it is currently an excellent means of reaching the Western Dales, running through the very heart of the district from Settle to Garsdale Head. Even by publication of this guide its future may have been decided. If the line is retained it will be due to the monumental efforts of its many thousands of friends; if it should be doomed, then there should be heads rolling off the Ribblehead Viaduct. Surely sanity must prevail?

The Skipton-Carnforth line also serves the extreme south of the area, with stations at Giggleswick and Clapham.

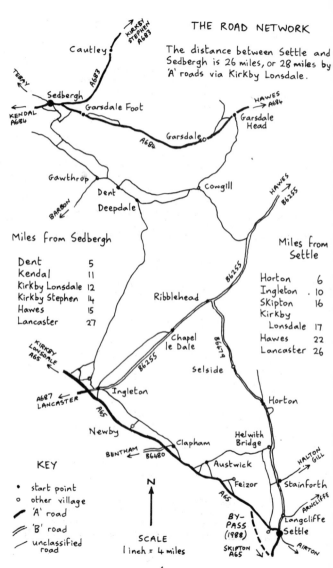

THE ROAD NETWORK

The distance between Settle and Sedbergh is 26 miles, or 28 miles by 'A' roads via Kirkby Lonsdale.

Cautley

KIRKBY STEPHEN A683

TEBAY

Sedbergh

KENDAL A684

Garsdale Foot

HAWES A684

Garsdale Head

Garsdale A684

Gawthrop

Dent

Cowgill

HAWES B6255

BARBON

Deepdale

Miles from Sedbergh

Dent	5
Kendal	11
Kirkby Lonsdale	12
Kirkby Stephen	14
Hawes	15
Lancaster	27

B6255

Ribblehead

Miles from Settle

Horton	6
Ingleton	10
Skipton	16
Kirkby Lonsdale	17
Hawes	22
Lancaster	26

Chapel le Dale

B6255

B6479

Selside

KIRKBY LONSDALE A65

A687 ← LANCASTER

Ingleton

A65

Horton

Newby

Helwith Bridge

HALTON GILL

KEY

- • start point
- ○ other village
- ⟍ 'A' road
- ⫽ 'B' road
- ⟋ unclassified road

BENTHAM B6480

Clapham

Austwick

Feizor

Stainforth

ARNCLIFFE

N

SCALE
1 inch = 4 miles

A65

BY-PASS (1988)

Langcliffe

Settle

SKIPTON A65

AIRTON

6

The 16 walks described range in length from $3\frac{3}{4}$ to 9 miles, and the terrain similarly varies from riverside strolls to rather more strenuous moorland walking. All are circular walks, and with an average distance of 6 miles they are ideally suited to half-day rambles. Each walk has its own chapter consisting of 'immediate impression' diagram and detailed narrative and strip-map, along with illustrations and notes of features of interest along the way.

Overleaf are listed the various facilities which are to be found in the area. There is a very good range of accommodation, which includes many of the inns. Some of these are in grand country settings, while only Settle, Ingleton Dent and Sedbergh can boast more than one. With only the odd exception they all sell traditional beer. On the transport scene, rail has already been mentioned, while bus services are very sparse in the northern half but reasonable in the south.

The area is well served by various information centres (see page 9), but many do not open during the winter months.

Local market days are as follows:
Settle - Tuesday
Sedbergh - Wednesday
Ingleton - Friday

ORDNANCE SURVEY MAPS

Although the strip-maps illustrating each walk are sufficient to guide one safely around, they cannot show the surrounding countryside. An Ordnance Survey map will, however, meet that need.

1:50,000 Landranger
sheet 98: Wensleydale and upper Wharfedale
sheet 97: Kendal and Morecambe (Walk 13 only)

1 inch to the mile
sheet 89: Lancaster and Kendal
sheet 90: Wensleydale

The area is also covered on only two maps at the 1:25,000 scale
OLM sheet 2: Yorkshire Dales - Western area
Pathfinder sheet 617: Sedbergh and Baugh Fell (SD 69/79)

SOME USEFUL FACILITIES

	Accommodation	Inn	Car park	Bus service	Rail service	Post Office	Other shop	Payphone	Campsite	WC
Austwick	✓	✓		✓		✓		✓		
Cautley	✓									
Chapel le Dale	✓	✓	✓			✓		✓		
Clapham	✓	✓	✓	✓	✓	✓	✓	✓		✓
Cowgill/Dent Head	✓	✓		*✓				✓	✓	
Deepdale Foot	✓							✓		
Dent	✓	✓	✓	✓		✓	✓	✓	✓	✓
Garsdale Head	✓			✓	✓			✓		
Gawthrop	✓					✓	✓			
Helwith Bridge	✓	✓		✓				✓	✓	
Horton	✓	✓	✓	✓	✓	✓	✓	✓	✓	✓
Ingleton	✓	✓	✓	✓		✓	✓	✓	✓	✓
Langcliffe	✓	✓	✓	✓		✓		✓	✓	
Ribblehead	✓	✓		*✓						
Sedbergh	✓	✓	✓	✓		✓	✓	✓	✓	✓
Settle	✓	✓	✓	✓	✓	✓	✓	✓		✓
Stainforth	✓	✓	✓	✓		✓	✓	✓	✓	✓

All known details are listed for the places visited on the walks. There are also youth hostels at Dent Head (Dentdale), Ingleton and Stainforth, and Dales Barns at Catholes Farm near Sedbergh and Dub Cote Farm, Horton. * The station near Cowgill is known as Dent, and that at Ribblehead is southbound only.

SOME USEFUL ADDRESSES

Ramblers' Association
1/5 Wandsworth Road, London SW8 2LJ
Tel. 01- 582 6878

Youth Hostels Association
Trevelyan House, St. Albans, Herts. AL1 2DY
Tel. St. Albans (0727) 55215

Yorkshire Dales National Park Office
Colvend, Hebden Road, Grassington
Skipton, North Yorkshire BD23 5LB
Tel. Grassington (0756) 752748

Clapham Information Centre - Car Park
Tel. Clapham (04685) 419

Sedbergh Information Centre - Main Street
Tel. Sedbergh (0587) 20125

Yorkshire and Humberside Tourist Board
312 Tadcaster Road, York YO2 2HF
Tel. York (0904) 707961

Tourist Information - Town Hall, Settle
Tel. Settle (07292) 3617
- Penyghent Cafe, Horton
Tel. Horton (07296) 333
- Community Centre Car Park, Ingleton
Tel. Ingleton (0468) 41049

Ribble Motor Services
Frenchwood Avenue, Preston PR1 4LU
Tel. Preston (0772) 54754

Pennine Motors
Main Street, Gargrave   Tel. Gargrave (075678) 215

D. Whaites,
12 High Hill Grove, Settle   Tel. Settle (07292) 3235

Yorkshire Dales Society
152 Main Street, Addingham, Ilkley,
West Yorkshire LS29 0LY

THE WALKS

Listed below are the 16 walks described, the walk number being the key to easy location in the guide.

THE WALKS

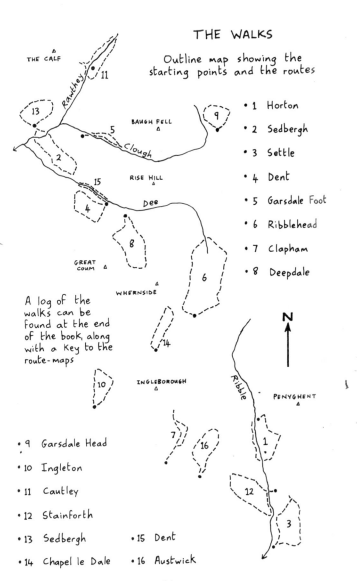

Outline map showing the
starting points and the routes

- 1 Horton
- 2 Sedbergh
- 3 Settle
- 4 Dent
- 5 Garsdale Foot
- 6 Ribblehead
- 7 Clapham
- 8 Deepdale

A log of the
walks can be
found at the end
of the book, along
with a Key to the
route-maps

- 9 Garsdale Head
- 10 Ingleton
- 11 Cautley
- 12 Stainforth
- 13 Sedbergh   - 15 Dent
- 14 Chapel le Dale   - 16 Austwick

WALK 1

6½ miles

THE HEART OF RIBBLESDALE

From Horton-in-Ribblesdale

An excellent way to appraise the varied features of the upper valley of the Ribble

Use the main car-park in the village centre

THE WALK

Leave the car-park by the footbridge at its northern end to by-pass the narrow road-bridges near the Crown Hotel. At once take a stile on the left to follow the Ribble downstream. We cling to its bank as far as Cragg Hill Farm, apart from a brief spell deflected by an enclosure containing the sewage works (preceded by a stile on the right as opposed to the obvious one straight ahead).

At the farm do not be tempted by a footbridge but remain with the river until the accompanying field boundary parts company, then head directly away from the Ribble to join a once-enclosed track which soon reverts to its original status. After passing another footbridge we go under the railway and out onto a lane. Turn left for a few minutes and with the inn at Helwith Bridge in sight take a stile to cross a field and emerge onto the road via the inn's car-park.

Cross the bridge to a junction and go left up the valley's main road a short distance before opting for a walled rough track up to the right. Follow this up to a fork and keep left to eventually emerge from confinement at a gate. From a gate at the next wall a crumbling wall reappears on the left, and within yards a level green fork takes us away from the main track. This new track leads down to a gate, but it is the stile in the bottom corner that takes us further. Descend to another stile to join a lane at Dub Cote Farm.

Turn right along this narrow byway to a

junction, then right again between the various buildings of Brackenbottom and circuitously around to Horton's little school. Though we are now back in the village, there is still another sight before finishing. Cross the footbridge and turn right, then fork left along a track which soon joins a similar walled track. Head right as far as a gate on the left 100 yards past a seat, and cross the field to another gate. Continue across to the prominent clump of trees marking the position of Brants Gill Head.

A stile in the wall right of the trees admits to the vicinity of the beck head, which is seen to better advantage by a scramble down the slope. Above and behind the beck is a stile in a wall: head directly away from it to a gate to join another walled track. This is Harber Scar Lane, which drops down into the village rather tidily by the front door of the inn.

Horton-in-Ribblesdale is the highest village in a valley which ends in the Irish Sea beyond Preston, and is the centre of the Three Peaks country. It is not particularly attractive, with a curious mixture of dwellings strung along the road. Horton's real attraction is its location, as the sight of countless boots being pulled on in its overfaced car park will testify. There is a true walkers atmosphere here, and the renowned cafe is the focal point: inside can be found the famous clocking-in machine where prospective Three Peakers start their day. Further up the road is the inn with two adjacent arched bridges, while at the southern end of the village is the church of St. Oswald. It displays Norman and 15th century work, and the solid-looking tower has leanings towards Pisa.

Horton church and Penyghent

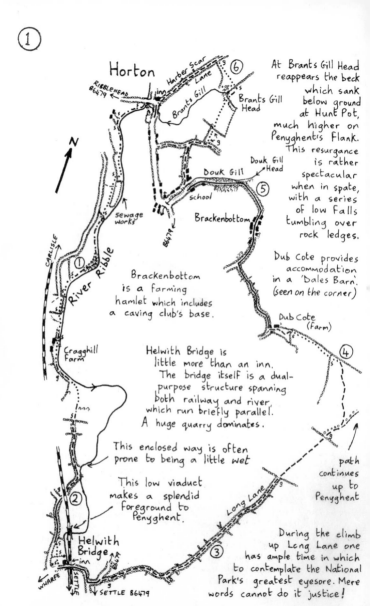

①

Horton

RIBBLEHEAD
B6479

Harber Scar Lane

Brants Gill

inn

⑥

Brants Gill
Head

At Brants Gill Head
reappears the beck
which sank
below ground
at Hunt Pot,
much higher on
Penyghent's Flank.
This resurgance
is rather
spectacular
when in spate,
with a series
of low falls
tumbling over
rock ledges.

Douk Gill
Head

Douk Gill

school

⑤

Brackenbottom

Dub Cote provides
accommodation
in a 'Dales Barn'.
(seen on the corner)

N

CARLISLE

River Ribble

sewage
works

B6479

①

Brackenbottom
is a farming
hamlet which includes
a caving club's base.

Dub Cote
(Farm)

④

Cragghill
Farm

Helwith Bridge is
little more than an inn.
The bridge itself is a dual-
purpose structure spanning
both railway and river,
which run briefly parallel.
A huge quarry dominates.

This enclosed way is often
prone to being a little *wet*

path
continues
up to
Penyghent

②

This low viaduct
makes a splendid
foreground to
Penyghent.

Long Lane

③

Helwith
Bridge

inn

B6479

WHARFE

SETTLE B6479

During the climb
up Long Lane one
has ample time in which
to contemplate the National
Park's greatest eyesore. Mere
words cannot do it justice!

14

WALK 2

FROSTROW FELLS AND MILLTHROP

$6\frac{3}{4}$ miles

From Sedbergh

Splendid mountain scenery from the feet of two valleys

looking north-east

Use either of Sedbergh's two car-parks

THE WALK

From the main street head east along the Kirkby Stephen road, soon forking right onto the Hawes road. At the first opportunity leave this also, by turning right along a narrow lane. Pass the first branch left, and at the next junction bear left up the 'no through road' which is Frostrow Lane. This is followed past several farms to its eventual demise alongside High Side farm. A stile in front empties onto the Frostrow Fells.

Follow the track heading directly away, soon becoming sketchy when the nearby wall parts company. Continue in the same direction, using the mound of Rise Hill (the continuation of our fell) as a guide. After nearing a wall-corner and a barn, a second wall-corner is reached with a beck just beyond it. The way improves here as it rises alongside the beck in the form of a sunken trod. As it peters out, keep rising to soon meet the wall marking the watershed.

Accompany this wall to the left for some time before arriving at a stile. The wall branching into Dentdale is followed only as far as a gate in it: now shadow the wall heading away again, through a gateway and then dropping more steeply towards the valley bottom. A track materialises to lead to a gate at the bottom left of this large pasture, then continues down to Helmside. From the gate on the left, cross the yard and use the short lane to join the road through Dentdale.

Head right along the road for three-quarters of a mile, and leave it at the second cluster of buildings after the crafts centre. Craggs Farm is easily identified as all its buildings stand on the left. Our way takes the gate just opposite, following a wall up to a stile then crossing a field to the farm buildings of Leakses. On joining its access-road go to the most distant building, a small barn with an adjacent gate. Several fields are now crossed, rising a little to Burton Hill farm. Pass between the buildings and up to a gate, then cross a field-bottom before aiming for Hewthwaite, the next farm. From a stile by the nearest building cross the access-track to a gate opposite. Two more fields are crossed to join another access-track, this time to Gap farm.

Pass along the front of the house, over a field and into a wood. The way is straightforward from here on. Enclosed for much of the way, our track leaves the wood to round the ridge-end towards Sedbergh. At a major fork keep right to a stile, joining a wide track winding down through a golf-course before becoming enclosed to enter Millthrop. Go right to a junction, and then left to join the road into Sedbergh. Cross the bridge to rise steadily back into the centre.

For a note on Sedbergh see page 52

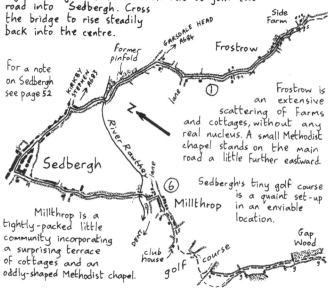

Frostrow is an extensive scattering of farms and cottages, without any real nucleus. A small Methodist chapel stands on the main road a little further eastward.

Sedbergh's tiny golf course is a quaint set-up in an enviable location.

Millthrop is a tightly-packed little community incorporating a surprising terrace of cottages and an oddly-shaped Methodist chapel.

Arrival above the golf course is a beautiful moment. In front are the Howgill Fells majestically dominating Sedbergh, with the Lune valley to the west: perfect in evening sunlight.

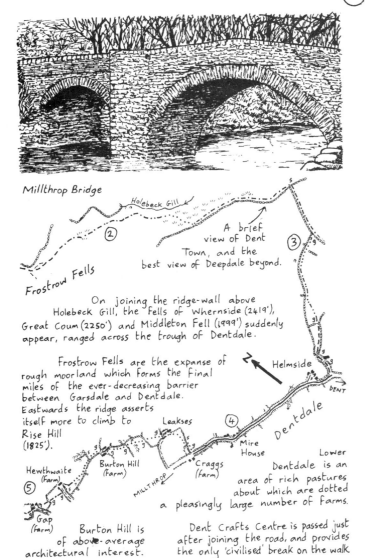

Millthrop Bridge

Holebeck Gill

(2)

A brief view of Dent Town, and the best view of Deepdale beyond.

(3)

Frostrow Fells

On joining the ridge-wall above Holebeck Gill, the Fells of Whernside (2419'), Great Coum (2250') and Middleton Fell (1999') suddenly appear, ranged across the trough of Dentdale.

Frostrow Fells are the expanse of rough moorland which forms the final miles of the ever-decreasing barrier between Garsdale and Dentdale. Eastwards the ridge asserts itself more to climb to Rise Hill (1825').

Helmside

N

DENT

Leakses

(4)

Dentdale

Mire House

Craggs (Farm)

MILLTHROP

Lower Dentdale is an area of rich pastures about which are dotted a pleasingly large number of farms.

Burton Hill (Farm)

Hewthwaite (Farm)

(5)

Gap (Farm)

Burton Hill is of above-average architectural interest.

Dent Crafts Centre is passed just after joining the road, and provides the only 'civilised' break on the walk

WALK 3

6¾ miles

CATRIGG FORCE AND THE SETTLE CAVES

from Settle

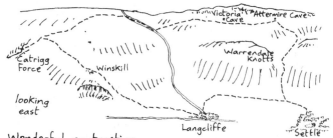

Catrigg Force · Winskill · Victoria Cave · Attermire Cave · Warrendale Knotts · Langcliffe · Settle

looking east

Wonderful contrasting natural scenery, from waterfall to cave.

There is ample parking in the centre of Settle

THE WALK

Leave the market-place by Constitution Hill, to the left of the Shambles. After a steep pull the lane turns left, and almost at once leave it along a rough track to the right. After a gate continue along the field bottom, using another gate to be briefly enclosed again before heading on to a stile on the left. Slope across to find another stile, then continue along with another left-hand wall, finally dropping left to a stile onto the lane just above Langcliffe.

Turn into the village and take the second lane on the right (opposite the green). Within a few yards is a little crossroads: head straight across and follow this enclosed track until its demise, there opting for the right-hand of two gates. Cross the field-top to a gate at the very end, then climb steeply above a former quarry to find a small gate in the top corner. Head up through a smaller pasture, and when a narrow track heads left, take a stile to its right, cutting a corner to another stile to rejoin the track. Turn right along it, and beyond a gate is the entrance to High Winskill.

Our way follows the track directly ahead, soon reaching a stile before petering out in the next field. Another stile soon appears ahead, and it is from here we make the detour to Catrigg Force. Its location is in no doubt, being enclosed in the trees at the bottom of the field. A pair of neighbouring stiles are the final obstacles, leading to the top of the waterfall, where with great care we are able to peer down to the bottom. The conventional view can be had by entering the trees on the left to descend a good path to the foot of the Force.

On returning to the stile at the top of the large field, go left along a farm-track which rises to join the road from Langcliffe to Malham Moor near a cattle-grid. Turn right along the verges of this unfenced strip of tarmac as far as the next cattle-grid, and from it strike left on a less-than clear track to rise to a stile in an intervening wall. After the outcrops beyond it turn left to another stile onto a wide track: up to the left are the conspicuous entrances of Jubilee Caves.

Follow the track right, leaving it at a gate and maintaining the same course on a path. After two stiles a path rises below a patch of scree to arrive at the enormous entrance to Victoria Cave. Another path returns us to the main one to resume the journey below a line of scars. After an open pasture Attermire Scar is reached, and the main path descends directly to a gateway. If wishing to explore Attermire Cave, do not descend but take a lesser path forking left and remaining level to arrive below the cave's modest entrance in the cliff just above. From it the gateway can be reached by descending a path across the scree.

Through the gateway follow the wall away, crossing a stile and rising to a gateway. An initially sketchy path bears right, passing a cave before arriving at a gap-stile by a gate. Descend to a wall-corner but then continue straight down a steep slope to rejoin the outward path: a left turn will lead in only a few minutes back into Settle's market-place.

Victoria
Cave

Jubilee Cave, looking out

Catrigg Force

Settle is a bustling little town which acts as a focal point for an extensive rural area comprising largely of upper Ribblesdale. It is invariably busy, being a long-established resting place for those bound farther afield, and is also an ideal centre for the Three Peaks country. Market days present the liveliest scene when the small square is covered with stalls.

Settle boasts numerous old buildings, some hidden and others very much on display. Facing the market square is a historic row known as the Shambles, with its shops peeping from behind archways. Nearby is a striking 17th century structure known as The Folly, a large rambling place.

Also facing the square is the 'Naked Man', a cafe with an appropriate carved sign dated 1633 and the source of some humour. Two museums are worth visiting, namely the Museum of North Craven Life and the privately owned Pig Yard Museum, which displays finds of archaeological interest from Victoria Cave. Soon Settle will be still more pleasant, with completion of a by-pass due in 1988.

Settle

CARLISLE
LANGCLIFFE
Banks Lane
A65 INGLETON
SKIPTON
A65 SKIPTON
KIRKBY MALHAM
N

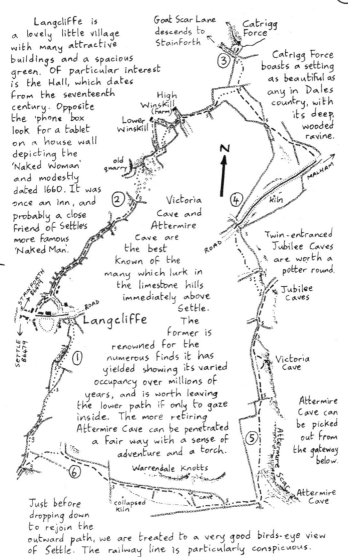

Langcliffe is a lovely little village with many attractive buildings and a spacious green. Of particular interest is the Hall, which dates from the seventeenth century. Opposite the 'phone box look for a tablet on a house wall depicting the 'Naked Woman' and modestly dated 1660. It was once an inn, and probably a close friend of Settle's more famous 'Naked Man'.

Goat Scar Lane descends to Stainforth

Catrigg Force

Catrigg Force boasts a setting as beautiful as any in Dales country, with its deep, wooded ravine.

High Winskill (Farm)

Lower Winskill

old quarry

MALHAM

N

KILN

ROAD

Twin-entranced Jubilee Caves are worth a potter round.

Jubilee Caves

STAINFORTH B6479

ROAD

Langcliffe

SETTLE B6479

Victoria Cave and Attermire Cave are the best known of the many which lurk in the limestone hills immediately above Settle. The former is renowned for the numerous finds it has yielded showing its varied occupancy over millions of years, and is worth leaving the lower path if only to gaze inside. The more retiring Attermire Cave can be penetrated a fair way with a sense of adventure and a torch.

Victoria Cave

Attermire Cave can be picked out from the gateway below.

Attermire Scar

Attermire Cave

Warrendale Knotts

CAVE

collapsed kiln

Just before dropping down to rejoin the outward path, we are treated to a very good birds-eye view of Settle. The railway line is particularly conspicuous.

WALK 4

5½ miles

Beckside and fellside walking combine to provide delightful close-hand and majestic distant views

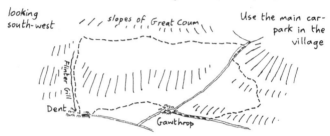

looking south-west — slopes of Great Coum — Use the main car-park in the village — Flinter Gill — Dent — Gawthrop

THE WALK

From the car-park cross the road and take the lane rising alongside the memorial Hall. It soon takes the form of a stony track, climbing parallel with Flinter Gill. On opening out it becomes enclosed by walls and pleasanter underfoot to join a wide green lane. Follow this to the right to eventually descend onto the Dent-Barbon road.

Accompany it briefly to the right before a footpath sign points the way through a gate on the left. A sketchy track crosses to a stile at the far corner. From it head towards the steep slope to the left: as it is reached a path appears and heads along to the right as a superb green promenade. All too soon a gate is reached and the track fades at the sad ruins of an old farm. Pass round the back and follow a barely-discernable wall heading away.

Down the field a farm-track is joined to head left down through a gateway. Amidst many crumbling walls it continues down to another gateway to approach Tofts. Before crossing the tree-lined beck in front of it however, leave the track to search for a slab footbridge a few yards downstream. The opposite bank is surmounted to reach the farm buildings. Pass between them and out along the access track to drop down gradually onto a lane. Gawthrop is only minutes along to the right.

The hamlet is vacated by the third branch

on the right after crossing the bridge (just after a phone box). The track swings left between houses: after crossing another beck fork right, but within yards take an enclosed path left in front of a short row of cottages to rejoin a wider track by a barn. Take the gate to its right and cross the tops of two fields and the centres of another two to descend to a track to the large cluster of farm buildings at Mill Beck.

    Remain on the track through several gates and continue to a gate by the last of the buildings. Now drop down a steep field half-left to a wall-corner, then use a gap on the right and cross a field bottom. In the next field take a stile immediately on the left to enter a field used as a caravan site. Head right to a farmyard, then on a track left to emerge onto the road adjacent to the Methodist chapel. The village centre is just along to the right.

Dent Town

On passing through the gate before the ruins of Combe House, the striking hollow of Combe Scar looms above. This colourful scene— unfairly bereft of rights-of-way— graces the northern flank of 1999' Middleton Fell. It is a popular Dentdale landmark with more than a hint of lakeland about it.

Gawthrop is a picturesque grouping of cottages and farms well off the beaten track.

For a note on the Occupation Road see page 36

Tofts

Combe House (ruin)

At Gawthrop

SEDBERGH

BARBON

Gawthrop

BARBON

DENT

At Gawthrop

Near the top of Flinter Gill we emerge from wooded confines and Middleton Fell appears across to the west. On joining the Occupation Road, the whole of lower Dentdale comes into view,

For a note on Dent see page 57

Dent

SEDBERGH

DEEPDALE

COWGILL

Flinter Gill

leading the eye unerringly to the splendid Howgill Fells.

Flinter Gill is a lively beck tumbling over a series of rock ledges in an enchanting wooded setting.

WALK 5

| LOWER GARSDALE |

6¼ miles

from Garsdale Foot

A modest stroll through the pastures of the lower valley. Giant fells overshadow impressively.

There is a large parking area on Longstone Common, 2½ miles out of Sedbergh where the Hawes road (A684) becomes unfenced.

THE WALK

From the car-park take the minor road dropping to Danny Bridge over the River Clough, and follow this traffic-free byway updale for a good mile and a half. Several farms are passed and several gates encountered: after a long spell of being open to the left we become fully enclosed again to descend to a farm on a right-angle bend. A little further along is a short, steep pull, just past which is a gate labelled 'Bellow Hill'. Follow the track through the field, but at the first wall strike right to a stile. Head on by the wall to cross a tiny beck, to see the only gap in the next wall being a gate down to the right. Now aim for the farm across the field, using a stile in front of it to join its lane which drops down to the road.

Go left along the road for a quarter-mile or so, taking greater care as this is now the main road, not the back lane, and the verges offer little refuge. At the allotted distance — just beyond the first farm on the right — look for a half-hidden stile on a bend (left side of the road). Follow the wall away from it to a stile in the corner, and locate the next stile just left of the barn in front. Cross the next field to a gateway and then on to a stile back onto the road. Head left once again, this time in happily wider confines. After a long quarter-mile take a stile just past a barn to descend to the now close-at-hand River Clough.

The return leg now begins: at the end of the first pasture a gate and some trees deflect us briefly from the river, but then a long, pleasant and straightforward walk

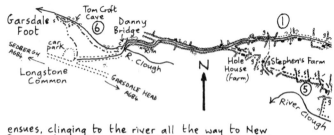

ensues, clinging to the river all the way to New
Bridge, where the main road crosses to its south bank.
Cross straight over the road and descend some steps to
continue downstream as far as the first field boundary. Here
a guidepost points us up to a barn. If its left-side is still
defended by shoulder-high nettles then keep to the track, rising
as far as the first bend above the barn. Now take a stile
on the left, crossing several fields to arrive at the front of
Stephen's Farm.

Continue across until Hole House farm appears just
beyond it, and cross to a gate at the right side of a tiny
plantation to enter its yard. Keep on past the buildings to
emerge back onto our outward lane which then returns us to
Danny Bridge. On crossing the bridge an enjoyable finish can
be incorporated by following the riverbank downstream on the
Sedgwick Geological trail. The trail ends beyond a short fenced
section, and an initially sketchy path rises across the common
and back to the car-park.

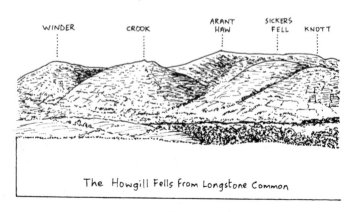

The Howgill Fells from Longstone Common

Garsdale is today probably the least known of any valley in the National Park, though the Norse settlers knew it well enough. Rather featureless hills rise steeply on either side, and more unhelpfully there are no rights-of-way up either fell for mile upon mile. The dale's 'centre' is a tiny community called The Street some way up the valley, and most people's only experience of Garsdale is through a car-window en route from Hawes to Sedbergh.

The very idea of a 'tourist attraction' in Garsdale seems to be breaking with tradition somewhat, but that, near enough, is what the well-designed Sedgwick Geological Trail is. Our walk concludes with a flourish by including the trail, which follows the River Clough downstream from Danny Bridge for a short distance on what is a permissive path.

The trail is named after the renowned geologist Adam Sedgwick (see page 57) and not after an imaginary nearby village as a new Dales guidebook would have us believe. A very detailed - beyond the author, to be honest- leaflet is available in Sedbergh or at the car-park explaining what to look for in this remarkable area, where the important Dent Fault is much in evidence.

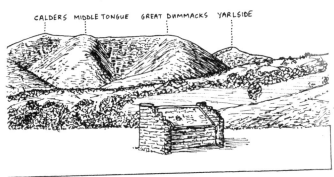

CALDERS   MIDDLE TONGUE   GREAT DUMMACKS   YARLSIDE

WALK 6

BLEA MOOR AND DENT HEAD

9 miles

from Ribblehead

An invigorating march through the
bleak country at the heads
of two valleys

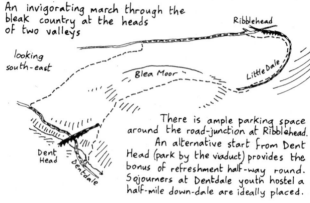

There is ample parking space
around the road-junction at Ribblehead.
An alternative start from Dent
Head (park by the viaduct) provides the
bonus of refreshment half-way round.
Sojourners at Dentdale youth hostel a
half-mile down-dale are ideally placed.

<u>THE WALK</u>

From the inn walk a few yards in the Hawes
direction then leave the road by the wide track heading
for the viaduct. Fork right just before its arches on a
reasonable path which runs parallel with the railway just
over the wall. This situation continues for quite some time,
though the path becomes damp underfoot and occasionally
less clear as Blea Moor signal-box is passed. At the second
bridge over the railway, just prior to Blea Moor tunnel,
cross it and follow a crudely-paved path up to a gate.
Here is a splendid view of the lower falls of Force Gill.
At this point the path is left and the fence is
followed right to a stile. Our route now traces the course
of the railway tunnel: descend to cross the trickle of
Little Dale Beck, while making for the prominent spoil-heap
just ahead. Here a good path is joined to rise up the
hillside past two more heaps and attendant air-shafts,
before levelling out to arrive at a stile in a boundary
fence with Dentdale now in front.
The path descends past another air-shaft and
through a plantation to meet the railway line again at
the northern entrance to its tunnel. From a stile drop down
by the left side of the line: the path soon moves away from
it through a gateway to cross a footbridge. Just a little

28

Further downstream the farmyard of Dent Head is entered through a pair of gates. Cross the bridge to the right of the buildings and head half-right across a large field. From a stile in the far bottom corner, follow the right-hand fence down to an attractive farm-bridge onto the road through Dentdale. With the equally-attractive cottage of Bridge End opposite, this is the most distant part of the walk.

To begin the return, head right up the steep and narrow road, and under an arch of Dent Head viaduct. Continue climbing the road and as it levels out beyond a milestone, a stile and guidepost on the right indicate the way back. An undulating track is now followed, sometimes sketchy and more than occasionally wet. Two fences are met in quick succession and the way soon improves into a pleasanter green track.

At a guidepost just before the first farm (High Gayle) fork right off the main track to run along the top of the intake-wall above the farm. When the wall drops away follow it down to the dwellings at Winshaw, and then out along the access-road onto the Ingleton-Hawes road at Far Gearstones.

Turn right along it for a long mile's walking back to Ribblehead, passing the buildings at Gearstones on the way. This road-walking is not as tortuous as might be expected, as much of the tarmac can be avoided in favour of the grass verge.

Ribblehead stands at the junction of two important Dales roads, where that from Ribblesdale meets the straight-as-a-die Ingleton to Hawes road. The only buildings here are the inn and some cottages by the railway. Ribblehead's nationally known feature, however, is its 24-arch viaduct which stands as a noble symbol of Victorian enthusiasm and engineering skills, but sadly also of the sheer folly and short-sightedness of our modern 'leaders'. Had they but a fraction of their fore-fathers' vision!

Batty Moss Viaduct

①

inn (cave)

INGLETON B6255 ←

Ribblehead

HORTON B6479 →

→ SETTLE

Force Gill boasts two fine waterfalls, and it is the lower of these that we see from the gate. The short section of paved path after the aqueduct is a modern effort designed to protect a route rapidly becoming over-used through the diversion of the 'Three Peaks' ascent of Whernside.

The main track is an old packhorse route known as the Craven Way. It continues over the hill into Dentdale.

Force Gill

Blea Moor Tunnel (south entrance)

air shafts

Blea Moor

aqueduct

Little Dale Beck

Blea Moor Siding

Hare Gill

On reaching the air shafts the view improves as Baugh Fell's appearance signals the opening out to the north. Blea Moor Tunnel is by far the longest tunnel on the Settle-Carlisle line. Constructed in the 1870's, it burrows under the moor for about 2630 feet. The central and deepest air shaft provides ventilation from more than 350 feet above the railway line.

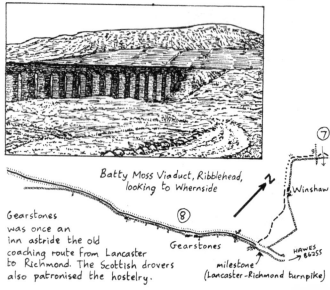

Batty Moss Viaduct, Ribblehead, looking to Whernside

N

Winshaw

(8)

Gearstones was once an inn astride the old coaching route from Lancaster to Richmond. The Scottish drovers also patronised the hostelry.

Gearstones

milestone (Lancaster-Richmond turnpike)

HAWES B6255

On attaining the Dentdale side of Blea Moor's bleak top, the panorama over the valley is marvellous. Beyond the foot of the dale is a lengthy lakeland skyline, with the rounded Howgill Fells nearer to hand. Nearer still is Rise Hill backed by Baugh Fell, with Wild Boar Fell and High Seat filling the gap to the right before nearby Widdale Fell closes in. Artengill Viaduct and Dent Station can also be picked out at the dale head.

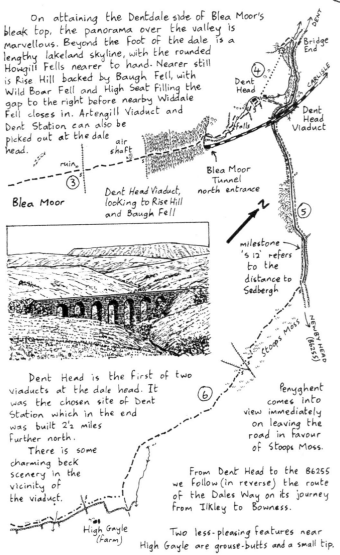

Blea Moor

Dent Head Viaduct, looking to Rise Hill and Baugh Fell

Blea Moor Tunnel north entrance

milestone 's 12' refers to the distance to Sedbergh

Dent Head is the first of two viaducts at the dale head. It was the chosen site of Dent Station which in the end was built 2½ miles further north.

There is some charming beck scenery in the vicinity of the viaduct.

Penyghent comes into view immediately on leaving the road in favour of Stoops Moss.

From Dent Head to the B6255 we follow (in reverse) the route of the Dales Way on its journey from Ilkley to Bowness.

Two less-pleasing features near High Gayle are grouse-butts and a small tip.

High Gayle (farm)

WALK 7

5¾ miles

GAPING GILL AND CLAPDALE

From Clapham

A straightforward
exploration of the
many interesting
limestone features
that lurk in the
fine valley above
Clapham.

Gaping
Gill

looking
north-west

Trow
Gill

Slapdale
Farm

Ingleborough
Cave

Clapham

Clapdale

Use the
National Park car-park
in the village centre

THE WALK

From the car-park cross the footbridge and take
the lane up to the top of the village. Just after it turns
left, a gate on the right leads to the cottage where modest
dues must be paid for the worthy pleasure of experiencing
the private grounds beyond. A wide track goes to the right
of the cottage then zig-zags up to the foot of the Lake.
This wide track is now followed unerringly past the numerous
features of this fascinating valley. Beyond Ingleborough Cave
a corner is rounded to climb through Trow Gill onto the
open moor. A good path accompanies a wall, crossing it
at the second stile reached. Just behind it is Bar Pot, and
a few minutes further the path leads a little sketchily
and damply to the unmistakeable hollow of Gaping Gill.

Having had a good-and cautious-potter about,
steps can be retraced to the wall and back down through
Trow Gill to Ingleborough Cave. A little further on, the
return can be varied by taking a path rising up to the
right just prior to entering Clapdale Wood. After a short
climb Clapdale Farm is reached: take the stile on the left
to enter its yard, then head directly away along its access
track.

Good views across Clapdale to the plateau of
Norber are enjoyed before the track descends (with views
ahead of the Bowland moors) to the edge of Clapham again,
emerging next to the ticket cottage. This varied finish can be
concluded by crossing the first bridge to approach the church,
then turning right to return to the car park.

Clapham is a beautiful village in a setting to match. Thankfully by-passed some years ago, it stands at the foot of Ingleborough from where the waters of Clapham Beck flow to form the centrepiece of the village. Several attractive bridges cross the tree-lined watercourse, and a splendid array of stone cottages line the parallel lane. On the east side of the beck are ranged all the individual features including the inn, the car park and National Park Centre - the old manor house - , the Cave Rescue Organisation HQ, and the church. Dedicated to St. James, its 15th century tower is the best feature.

Near the church is Ingleborough Hall, currently an outdoor centre, but formerly the home of the Farrer family. Best known of them was Reginald (1880 - 1920) who found fame as a botanist, collecting alpine plants on his journeys to far-flung parts and bringing many back to the grounds of the hall. The heavily-wooded grounds and the lake were created by the family earlier in the 19th century. The estate is still privately-owned, hence the small admission fee for enjoying the grounds.

Trow Gill

Gaping Gill

Gaping Gill is the great hole, the one that everyone has heard of and that a good number of non-cavers have descended. On the open moor in the lap of Ingleborough, this mighty chasm cannot fail to impress. The innocuous stream of Fell Beck suddenly falls an unbroken 340 feet from the unfenced lip to the floor of the chamber, which is said to be of sufficient size to hold York Minster. This is no place for skylarking or unrestrained children.

At the two main bank holiday weekends one of two local caving clubs set up a chair and winch to lower the likes of you and me down. If not charged for the descent, you'll have to pay to return to the surface! Several miles of passages radiate from the main chamber, and the course of Fell Beck finally returns to daylight as Clapham Beck, at Beck Head alongside Ingleborough Cave. A connection by cavers was only established in the 1980's after many years efforts.

For the experienced and well-prepared Gaping Gill can be used as a springboard for the ascent of mighty Ingleborough, which looks most inviting in the right conditions.

The wonders of Clapdale include Trow Gill, a former cave and now an overhanging ravine, Gordale in style if not in proportions: unlike Gordale, its valley is dry. Ingleborough Cave is a show cave with guided tours, at least requiring a worthwhile walk to reach it.

In the charming estate grounds is the Grotto, a useful shelter in rain, but the water that will be appreciated is that of the Lake, an artificial tarn locked in glorious woodland.

Fell Beck
Gaping Gill
Disappointment Pot
Bar Pot ③
N
Trow Gill ②
Foxholes
Beck Head
Ingleborough Cave
Clapdale Farm
Clapdale Drive ④
Clapdale Wood
The Grotto ①
⑤
Clapdale Lane
Clapham Beck
INGLETON
The Lake
waterfall
Ingleborough Hall
car park
inn
SETTLE
Clapham

WALK 8

6½ miles

A CIRCUIT OF DEEPDALE

from Deepdale Foot

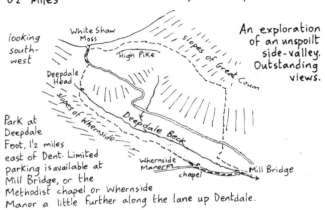

looking south-west

An exploration of an unspoilt side-valley. Outstanding views.

Park at Deepdale Foot, 1½ miles east of Dent. Limited parking is available at Mill Bridge, or the Methodist chapel or Whernside Manor a little further along the lane up Dentdale.

THE WALK

Take the farm lane rising alongside the Methodist chapel and remain on it until a sharp bend just beyond some barns. Here take the gate in front and continue the same course across the top of a field to an almost-hidden stile at the far end. Keep by a fence just above Deepdale Beck, and from the next stile several fields are crossed with stiles always there to confirm the way. Eventually a wall joins from the left to lead us to Mire Garth Farm.

Continue by the wall to a ruin, and from the stile to its right head past a barn to reach the gate to Deepdale Head farm. Instead of this gate take the smaller one a few yards beyond. A corner of the farmyard is crossed to another gate, from where a steep climb ensues alongside a tiny beck on the right. From a stile at the top a path runs to a guidepost, and from it head half-right, guided by posts up the open pasture. A small but conspicuous gully is the key to a stile just to its left, and here the Ingleton-Dent road is joined close to its summit.

Turn up the road a short distance and then leave it by a walled track to the right. Apart from one brief spell without walls, the way is completely foolproof

Whernside Manor was built about two hundred years ago when it was known as West House. It is now in the hands of the National Park Authority, and its proper title is the National Park Outdoor Recreation and Study Centre. Having initially specialised in caving, it now runs a range of courses in various outdoor activities.

Nun House Outrake is a Jekyll and Hyde character, partly a delight, partly like a stony river bed.

Deepdale Methodist chapel stands in a typically isolated location, tucked hard by a lane junction embowered in trees.

The Occupation Road is a walled track which runs across the northern flank of Great Coum, linking the Dent-Ingleton road with that from Gawthrop to Barbon. An old packhorse way, it provides marvellous views from its strictly defined contour.

THE WALK *continued*
as it winds its level course round the hillside under the shadow of the nearby summit of Great Coum. When another walled track presents an opportunity to leave, take it and follow it all the way down onto the Ingleton-Dent road once more.

Cross straight over and down a short track, crossing over a wider track and across a small field behind. From a gate at the far side descend by a hedge to a gate above some barns. Drop left to a stile by the nearest building and then commence a level course along to the left. At the end of the meadow is a stile near Deepdale Beck: continue on past a small limekiln, rising a little to the next field above a line of trees.

From the next stile head on below a short length of wall, then bear right to the trees shrouding the beck. A path descends to it to reach Mill Bridge only yards further downstream. Cross the bridge and the chapel will be found only a couple of minutes up to the right.

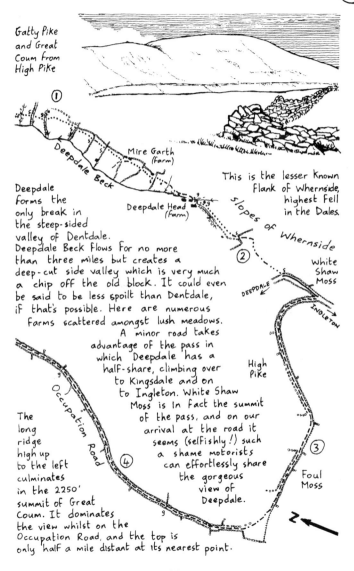

Gatty Pike and Great Coum from High Pike

① Deepdale Beck
Mire Garth (Farm)
Deepdale Head (Farm)

This is the lesser known flank of Whernside, highest fell in the Dales.

slopes of Whernside

② DEEPDALE
White Shaw Moss
INGLETON

High Pike

③ Foul Moss

Occupation Road ④

N ←

Deepdale forms the only break in the steep-sided valley of Dentdale. Deepdale Beck flows for no more than three miles but creates a deep-cut side valley which is very much a chip off the old block. It could even be said to be less spoilt than Dentdale, if that's possible. Here are numerous farms scattered amongst lush meadows.

A minor road takes advantage of the pass in which Deepdale has a half-share, climbing over to Kingsdale and on to Ingleton. White Shaw Moss is in fact the summit of the pass, and on our arrival at the road it seems (selfishly!) such a shame motorists can effortlessly share the gorgeous view of Deepdale.

The long ridge high up to the left culminates in the 2250' summit of Great Coum. It dominates the view whilst on the Occupation Road, and the top is only half a mile distant at its nearest point.

WALK 9

3¾ miles

| GRISEDALE AND TURNER HILL |

from Garsdale Head

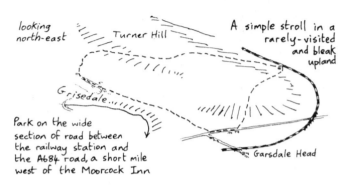

looking north-east

Turner Hill

A simple stroll in a rarely-visited and bleak upland

Grisedale

Park on the wide section of road between the railway station and the A684 road, a short mile west of the Moorcock Inn

Garsdale Head

THE WALK

Take the road down to the T-junction and cross straight over the main road to a stile. Head up the pasture to the next stile, from where the waterfall of Clough Force can be seen down to the left by a detour towards the beck. Back on the hillside continue in a near-straight line towards Grisedale. A prominent tree entices us towards a group of farm buildings, and from a stile to the right, several more lead us down into the valley. Without joining the road at Beck Side, take a stile just beyond some barns and continue parallel with the road, and use another stile near a barn to emerge onto the unenclosed road at Moor Rigg.

Turn right to the road's demise at East House, then continue up the track onto the open moor. Fork right by the intake wall, and when the track fades curve gently left on a level course to a gate in view well ahead. From it descend a rough pasture to a footbridge over the railway line. Do not cross it but take a stile between the line and the lone house, and head diagonally across to a collapsed wall. Rising behind it, use a depression between two gentle slopes to locate a stile in the next wall. Now a sketchy path continues across two pastures before beginning a direct descent to the main road, emerging at a stile opposite a farm.

The Garsdale Head road junction is now only a couple of minutes along to the right.

Swarth Fell from Blake Mire

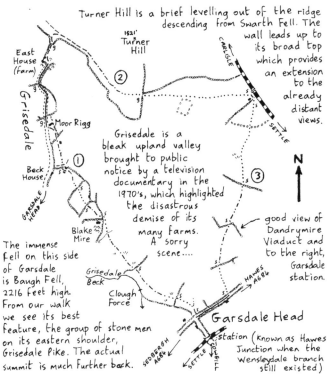

Turner Hill is a brief levelling out of the ridge descending from Swarth Fell. The wall leads up to its broad top which provides an extension to the already distant views.

1521' Turner Hill

East House (farm)

Moor Rigg

Beck House

Griesdale

② ③

CARLISLE

SETTLE

N

good view of Dandrymire Viaduct and to the right, Garsdale station.

Grisedale is a bleak upland valley brought to public notice by a television documentary in the 1970's, which highlighted the disastrous demise of its many farms. A sorry scene....

Blake Mire

GARSDALE HEAD

The immense fell on this side of Garsdale is Baugh Fell, 2216 feet high. From our walk we see its best feature, the group of stone men on its eastern shoulder, Grisedale Pike. The actual summit is much further back.

Grisedale Beck

Clough Force

Garsdale Head

HAWES A684

station (known as Hawes Junction when the Wensleydale branch still existed)

SEDBERGH A684

SETTLE

CARLISLE

39

WALK 10

4¼ miles

A classic, and rightly so.
Don't go after
a prolonged
drought.

| THE INGLETON GLENS |

from Ingleton

Descend the steep road
by the church, and
the entrance and
car-park are to
be found at the
second bridge.

Note for the financially
embarrassed: this walk
is over private land and
requires a payment at the start.

looking
north-
west

THE WALK

Few directions are needed for this walk, as the paths
are very clear throughout, and the way obvious: from the car
park the path heads up the valley of the Twiss, twice crossing
the river to arrive at Pecca Falls. A little further is Thornton
Force, beyond which the path soon crosses the beck to rise to
an enclosed track. This is Twisleton Lane, which leads along to
the right to the confines of Twisleton Hall Farm. Keep left of all
the buildings, using two stiles and a track which descends a field
to a lane. Cross straight over and down to Beezleys Farm, going
between the buildings to a gate on the left.

A left fork leads to Beezley Falls, from where the
River Doe is now accompanied downstream. Beyond Snow Falls a
footbridge conveys us to the opposite bank, and our path rises
through trees, emerging high above the river at Cat Leap Force.
The path meets the head of a lane to enter the centre of
Ingleton. Turn right, and beyond the church drop down to cross
both rivers before reaching the car park.

Commonly referred to as the 'waterfalls walk', this
is one of the two famous excursions available from Ingleton
village, the other being the climb to the summit of Ingleborough.
With much justification, the falls walk has attracted visitors
for over a century, and probably more so than any other walk
in this book, it is worth savouring in one of the winter months
when the jostling has ceased. The paths are everywhere well
maintained – justifying the charge – but care is still needed when
wet leaves carpet the ground. Be also aware that, for a low-
level walk, there is a fair amount of 'up and down' work.

The two valleys explored on this walk are remarkably alike, each beautifully wooded and exposing interesting geological features, with the Craven Faults much in evidence. Even without the chief attractions, this would still be a fine walk. For some reason the names of the watercourses have caused confusion. The Twiss is known by some as the Greta, while more curiously Wainwright has transposed the Greta (Twiss) and the Doe. Maybe there's hope for the author yet! What is less in doubt is that at their meeting, if not any earlier, the Greta is born.

Above Thornton Force lies the flat valley floor of Kingsdale, at one time a glacial lake held back by Raven Ray, a good example of a moraine.

Ingleton is famed as the centre for Yorkshire's limestone country, and is certainly a good base for exploring the fells, scars, caves and valleys of the area. The roadside signs proclaiming 'Beauty Spot of the North' may raise the odd smile, but usually only from travellers on the busy A65 which avoids the village centre and its nearby attractions.

The centre of Ingleton is dominated by a long-abandoned railway viaduct. Also prominent is the parish church, and there are numerous interesting little corners to the village. The youth hostel is centrally situated, as are several useful hostelries and shops.

From the vicinity of Scar End, Ingleborough displays itself proudly

The 'beauty' of Ingleton, however, must be its location.

Thornton Force

WALK 11

6¼ miles

CAUTLEY SPOUT AND THE RAWTHEY

from Cautley

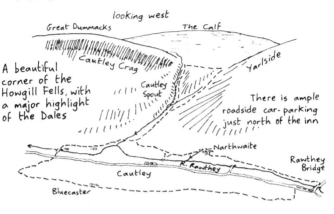

looking west

Great Dummacks   The Calf

Cautley Crag   Yarlside

A beautiful corner of the Howgill Fells, with a major highlight of the Dales

Cautley Spout

There is ample roadside car-parking just north of the inn

Narthwaite

Rawthey Bridge

Cautley   R. Rawthey

Bluecaster

THE WALK

From the parking space by the inn cross the footbridge over the Rawthey and go straight ahead to join a wide track. Turn right along it to a ford across Backside Beck, and from the gate behind it the track rises to the confines of Narthwaite. Leave the farm buildings by the access-track on the right, which is followed almost to the main road. A gate on a sharp bend just before it points us on a lesser track which ends at a wood. Ford the stream below it and cross the field to a fence. Step over it and follow the Rawthey upstream, passing through a wood and then fields to cross a tiny stream before rising onto the road just above Rawthey Bridge.

Cross the bridge and after a few yards take a gate on the left. A track heads away, almost immediately turning sketchily right at a damp section. Soon this track improves and after a gentle rise runs parallel with but high above the main road. Shortly after passing Bluecaster farm a gate is reached: just after it take one on the right to descend a sunken track (initially unclear) onto the road.

Head straight over the main road and along a wide farm-track over the river and through several fields to Cautley Thwaite farm. Keep straight on through a gate and alongside a wall before crossing to a barn. Stay right of

43

it to emerge onto a good path. Go right to Cautley Holme Beck, turning upstream to a footbridge from where a path on the far bank leads up to the foot of Cautley Spout. From this point there is a choice of either simply gazing up at the Spout and Cautley Crag, or having a closer look by taking the steep path by the gill.

After pausing at the main fall continue to the upper fall, much easier to appreciate for its lack of all-embracing foliage. By the top of it our path levels out, but here leave it by a trod going right. This slopes across the hillside, becoming sketchy to drop to the unmistakeable col of Bowderdale Head. Turn right to descend a good path by a beck, soon rejoining our outward path by the foot of the Spout. Return along the path this time passing the little bridge over Cautley Holme Beck and going upstream by the Rawthey. Soon the footbridge which began this ramble is reached, and now it is used to conclude the walk.

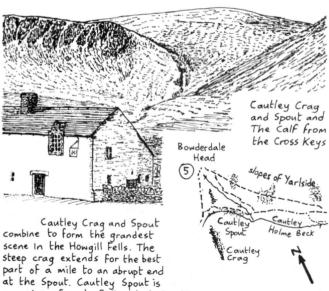

Cautley Crag and Spout and The Calf from the Cross Keys

Bowderdale Head

⑤ slopes of Yarlside

Cautley Spout

Cautley Holme Beck

Cautley Crag

N

Cautley Crag and Spout combine to form the grandest scene in the Howgill Fells. The steep crag extends for the best part of a mile to an abrupt end at the Spout. Cautley Spout is a series of waterfalls which tumble in rapid succession over a drop of hundreds of feet to the valley floor. The lower falls are draped with and partially obscured by some hardy foliage.

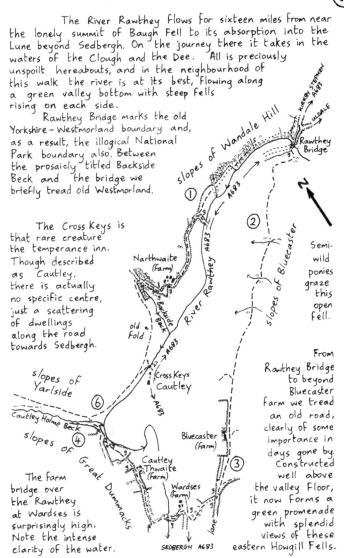

The River Rawthey flows for sixteen miles from near the lonely summit of Baugh Fell to its absorption into the Lune beyond Sedbergh. On the journey there it takes in the waters of the Clough and the Dee. All is preciously unspoilt hereabouts, and in the neighbourhood of this walk the river is at its best, flowing along a green valley bottom with steep fells rising on each side.

Rawthey Bridge marks the old Yorkshire - Westmorland boundary and, as a result, the illogical National Park boundary also. Between the prosaicly titled Backside Beck and the bridge we briefly tread old Westmorland.

The Cross Keys is that rare creature the temperance inn. Though described as Cautley, there is actually no specific centre, just a scattering of dwellings along the road towards Sedbergh.

Semi-wild ponies graze this open fell.

From Rawthey Bridge to beyond Bluecaster farm we tread an old road, clearly of some importance in days gone by. Constructed well above the valley floor, it now forms a green promenade with splendid views of these eastern Howgill Fells.

The farm bridge over the Rawthey at Wardses is surprisingly high. Note the intense clarity of the water.

KIRKBY STEPHEN A683
UldALE
Rawthey Bridge
slopes of Wandale Hill
①
②
A683
slopes of Bluecaster
River Rawthey
Narthwaite (Farm)
Backside Beck
old Fold
slopes of Yarlside
⑥
Cautley Holme Beck
④
slopes of Great Dummacks
Cross Keys Cautley
Bluecaster (Farm)
③
Cautley Thwaite (Farm)
Wardses (Farm)
lane
SEDBERGH A683

WALK 12 | SMEARSETT SCAR, FEIZOR AND THE RIBBLE |

7½ miles

from Stainforth

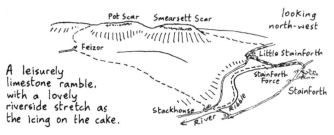

Pot Scar   Smearsett Scar

looking
north-west

Feizor

Little Stainforth

Stainforth
Force

Stainforth

Stackhouse

River Ribble

A leisurely
limestone ramble,
with a lovely
riverside stretch as
the icing on the cake.

Use the main car-park just off the main road

THE WALK:

From the car-park join the main road alongside
the village and turn right, leaving it almost immediately
by a lane to the left. The railway line is bridged before
descending to cross Stainforth Bridge then up to a junction
at Little Stainforth. Head along the lane to the right,
and at a bend take a track rising to a barn on the left.
The right-of-way is officially the parallel enclosed way, joining
the track above the barn. On rounding a wall-corner a
stile is found, and when the track suddenly ends continue
by the wall, the way being made clear by a string of four
further stiles in the same direction. From the last one no
more are visible: here continue straight across over the gentle
brow, with the steep slope on the left rising towards the
Ordnance column atop Smearsett Scar.

With no public right-of-way to the top, the route
simply crosses the pasture to the next stile. Intermittently it
heads half-right to another stile then remains by the wall
to reach a stile onto the lane through Feizor Nick. Go left
along it to descend into the heart of Feizor.

Follow the lane only to the cobbled watersplash,
then take a rough track on the left between barns. Beyond
a gate a wide track heads across a long pasture, continuing
sketchily when the accompanying wall leaves us. Eventually a
stile is reached, and the still-sketchy track maintains its
direction through two gates. Just past the second take a
gate on the right before resuming the trek. Beyond the

next gate the track zig-zags down to a gate where it fades completely. Head straight across the field where a choice of neighbouring stiles precede a steeper drop to the outside of Stackhouse's private world. Go right, and a sketchy path through the trees leads to a stile onto a lane.

Turn left past two entrances to Stackhouse and take an enclosed track to the right to meet the Ribble at the Locks. Don't use the footbridge but follow the river upstream: at the end of a long pasture after Langcliffe paper mill we are briefly parted from the river, but other than that its bank leads unerringly to Stainforth Force. Just above the falls is the packhorse bridge, from where the first few steps of the walk can be retraced up into Stainforth village.

Knight Stainforth Hall

Feizor is an unspoilt settlement at the terminus for motor vehicles of a short cul-de-sac to this hollow in the hills.

Footpaths, however, radiate in various directions.

Note the water pump and trough sited on the little green in front of the prettiest grouping of cottages.

Feizor Nick

N

Pot Scar

③

Feizor

TO A65

Smearsett Scar is the brother of Pot Scar, and boasts a shapely aspect when seen from the east (around Stainforth) or the west. Its south face falls away sharply with low crags giving way to scree slopes. Smearsett's character is rivalled admirably by its status as a viewpoint, and is probably the best vantage point for surveying Ribblesdale.

②

Pot Scar forms a striking backdrop to the cottages of Feizor, its gleaming scars apparently reaching for the sky.

④

Included are Horton and Helwith Bridge backed by Plover Hill, Penyghent and Fountains Fell. Then come Stainforth Scar and Settle's shapely hills. To the south are the Happy Valley and the Celtic Wall both close at hand and contrasting with distant Pendle Hill. Moving westwards are the Bowland Fells, and closer again we have Norber, Moughton, Ingleborough and a tip of Whernside.

Penyghent From Feizor Nick

Stainforth is a sizeable village stood high above and back from the Ribble, and by-passed some years ago by the main road up the dale. In central locations are a pleasant inn and the mid-nineteenth century church of St. Peter. Stainforth's best-known features, however, are outside the village. The hand of man fashioned an eighteenth century mansion on the Horton road, which now serves as a youth hostel, and also Stainforth Bridge, a graceful structure which conveyed the packhorse trade over the Ribble on the old York-Lancaster route. It is now in the care of the National Trust. Only 100 yards downstream are the beautifully sparkling falls.

1191' Smearset Scar

HELWITH BRIDGE

HORTON & A64 CARLISLE

Stainforth

SETTLE

Little Stainforth, also known as Knight Stainforth, is a tiny hamlet, and a kid brother to Stainforth across the river. Very noteworthy is the rather austere hall, dating largely from the mid-seventeenth century, and on the site of an older hall.

Little Stainforth

Hall

caravan site

STACKHOUSE

Stainforth Force

SETTLE & A65

Car Park

An easy but harmless error is to continue along the north side of this wall, a short detour which, by mishap or design, is most fruitful for the view of Penyghent from the outcrops there.

River Ribble

N

Stackhouse is a cosy little grouping of rather superior dwellings, huddling beneath the hill and happy to remain half-hidden in its protective surround of greenery.

paper mill

Stackhouse

an attractive scene

weir Locks

↓ SETTLE

WALK 13

4 miles

From Sedbergh

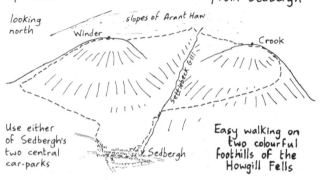

looking north

Use either of Sedbergh's two central car-parks

Easy walking on two colourful foothills of the Howgill Fells

THE WALK

Leave the main street by Joss Lane alongside the car-park. It rises past houses to a gate, there becoming a farm-track. Cross to the top corner of the field where a path climbs to run parallel with Settlebeck Gill, and a gate admits to the open fell. From a choice of paths take the least obvious one running down to the beck, which is forded just above the waterfall. The steep slope behind conceals a sunken track which rises sketchily to the high-point of the intake-wall. Take the good path sloping to the right across the face of Crook. It is well-graded throughout, and soon after swinging left above the valley of Ashbeck Gill a fork is met. Take the sunken way climbing left, and when it peters out the cairn atop Crook should be visible a little up to the left.

From Crook's top its brother Winder appears: as a bee-line is clearly out of the question, aim for the top of Settlebeck Gill, gaining a little height on the way. Cross the marshy beginnings of the beck and a parallel path before a gentle rise to the ridge running down to Winder from Arant Haw. A wide track is joined and despite a couple of forks the way to the Ordnance column on Winder is clear, only a modest ascent being required.

Leave the top by a path running west. It merges with another to descend to just above the intake-wall. Turn left above some trees to locate a narrow path through bracken. After Sedbergh appears the wall is joined: at a gate drop down through Lockbank farm onto Howgill Lane, turning left to re-enter Sedbergh.

The Howgill Fells are a compact, well-defined mountain group which must be suffering something of an identity crisis. Half the massif is in the Dales National Park, while half is not. Half was in the old county of Westmorland, half was in the West Riding of Yorkshire: since 1974 the entire group became part of Cumbria. To cap it all, these fells are alien to the Dales landscape and are more akin to Lakeland, whose National Park boundary is only 6 miles distant at one point. Wherever they are, or should be, there is no doubt that all the Howgills merit inclusion in a National Park.

Winder and Crook are two foothills of the group overlooking Sedbergh, with Winder in particular being a much trodden short climb. The Howgills rise to 2219 feet, are smooth, rounded and best of all free from walls and fences, leaving much freedom to roam.

Winder and Crook both claim excellent views of much of the Dales. At their feet is Sedbergh presiding over a complex meeting of valleys. The descent gives good views of the Lune Gorge and the western Howgills.

this path continues to the summit of the group

How gill Fells

Settlebeck Gill

▲ 1505'
CROOK

② ①

WINDER ▲ 1551'
O.S. col. SS659

falls

③

semi-wild ponies may be spotted roaming these slopes.

The path across the breast of Crook follows the course of a pipeline

HOWGILL

Lockbank Farm

Hill Farm

This road is Howgill Lane, which skirts the western base of the Howgill Fells on its way to the Lune Gorge.

KENDAL A684 ←

DENT ↓

KIRKBY STEPHEN A683 →
HAWES A684 →

Sedbergh

N ↑

Sedbergh is the largest community in the Yorkshire Dales National Park, yet its isolation has helped it avoid the excesses of commercialism. Ceded to Cumbria in 1974, Sedbergh – omit the last two letters in pronunciation – was previously in the north-western extremity of the West Riding of Yorkshire, incredibly over 100 miles distant from its West Riding colleague Sheffield. Two simple facts prove that size is very much a relative thing.

This tiny market town boasts an unparalleled position on the lower slopes of its 'own' mountains the Howgill Fells, and the outlook on three sides is, in fact, of fells. This is the edge of the Dales, and to the west of the town runs the River Lune. In the neighbourhood of Sedbergh three lively rivers end their journeys, as the Dee, Clough and Rawthey join forces to swell the waters of the Lune.

Aside from the imposing Howgill Fells, Sedbergh itself is dominated by its public school. This famous establishment, which was founded in the early 16th century, includes Adam Sedgwick (see page 57) among its old boys. The oldest remaining part dates from 1716, and is now the library. Most other features of interest will be found on or near the lengthy main street, including a lovely parish church in an equally attractive wooded surround. Dedicated to St. Andrew it has a 15th century tower, with other parts dating back to Norman times as well as many other periods in between.

St. Andrew's
Sedbergh

WALK 14 | THE ENVIRONS OF CHAPEL-LE-DALE

5¼ miles — from Chapel-le-Dale

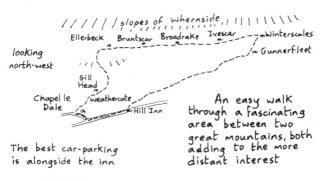

looking north-west

The best car-parking is alongside the inn

An easy walk through a fascinating area between two great mountains, both adding to the more distant interest

THE WALK

From the Hill Inn head south along the Ingleton road, turning off to the right within minutes on a lane into the trees. At the church fork right again up an inviting lane: it is a farm road and is followed without deviation, passing along the front of Gill Head before crossing a large pasture to Ellerbeck. A rougher track passes in front of the buildings to a gate, crosses a field, and then runs through a long narrow pasture to Bruntscar.

Just beyond the buildings leave the farm road and go straight ahead to a gate. Across the next pasture Broadrake is reached. Once again pass along the front, and a less-clear path leads through several fields to join a track to Ivescar. Head straight on again - with the bulk of the buildings on the right - on another farm road until just short of Winterscales, where a branch right takes us across a pasture to Gunnerfleet.

Do not cross the beck to it, but remain on the farm road through more fields before it decides to cross the beck. Leave it after a cattle-grid soon after the bridge, a sketchy path following the wall to a gate. Head away from it with the left-hand wall, and when it departs continue on to descend to witness the disappearance of Winterscales Beck.

Cross to the stile opposite and follow the wall away. At a gate enter an enclosed track on the left which emerges onto another farm road. Follow it left past Philpin and out onto the main road only yards below the Hill Inn.

The Hill Inn, Chapel-le-Dale, and Ingleborough

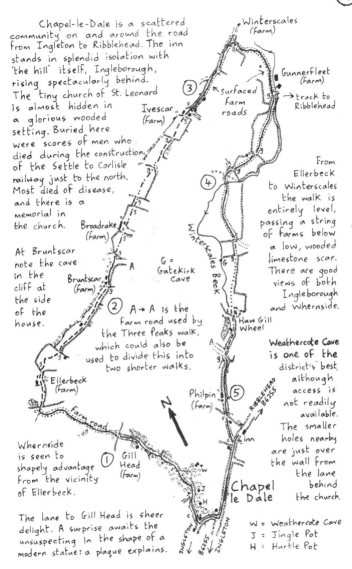

Chapel-le-Dale is a scattered community on and around the road from Ingleton to Ribblehead. The inn stands in splendid isolation with 'the hill' itself, Ingleborough, rising spectacularly behind. The tiny church of St. Leonard is almost hidden in a glorious wooded setting. Buried here were scores of men who died during the construction of the Settle to Carlisle railway just to the north. Most died of disease, and there is a memorial in the church.

At Bruntscar note the cave in the cliff at the side of the house.

Winterscales (farm)

Gunnerfleet (Farm)

→ track to Ribblehead

③ ←surfaced farm roads

Ivescar (Farm)

④

From Ellerbeck to Winterscales the walk is entirely level, passing a string of farms below a low, wooded limestone scar. There are good views of both Ingleborough and Whernside.

Broadrake (Farm)

G = Gatekirk Cave

Bruntscar (Farm)

Winterscales Beck

② A→A is the farm road used by the Three Peaks walk, which could also be used to divide this into two shorter walks.

Haw Gill Wheel

A

Weathercote Cave is one of the district's best, although access is not readily available. The smaller holes nearby are just over the wall from the lane behind the church.

Ellerbeck (Farm)

Philpin (Farm)

⑤

RIBBLEHEAD B6255

N

Farm road

Whernside is seen to shapely advantage from the vicinity of Ellerbeck.

① Gill Head (Farm)

inn

Chapel le Dale

W

J

H

The lane to Gill Head is sheer delight. A surprise awaits the unsuspecting in the shape of a modern statue: a plaque explains.

INGLETON B6255 INGLETON

W = Weathercote Cave
J = Jingle Pot
H = Hurtle Pot

WALK 15

4¾ miles

looking south-west

Dent
Barth Bridge
Ellers
R. Dee

THE BANKS OF THE DEE

From Dent

A simple riverside
stroll of peace and charm

Use the
main car
park in the
village

THE WALK

From the car-park head along the cobbled street and out by the main up-dale road to church Bridge across the Dee. Do not use it but take a stile to descend to the riverbank. The river is hugged almost all the way to the walks turning-point, the footbridge at Ellers. The only breaks are firstly early on when the Dee nudges us onto the road for a few yards, and secondly approaching Barth Bridge, where stiles take a more direct course onto the road. The riverside path resumes straight across the road.

On reaching the wooden footbridge at Ellers, cross it and cling to the opposite bank until forced up to the road by the Elam monument. Turn right for a short stroll back to Barth Bridge, then take the enclosed byway heading straight on by the river. The Dee moves away, and forks to two farms are passed before a stile returns us to the river for the final yards back to Church Bridge. Now it can be crossed to re-enter Dent.

Church Bridge

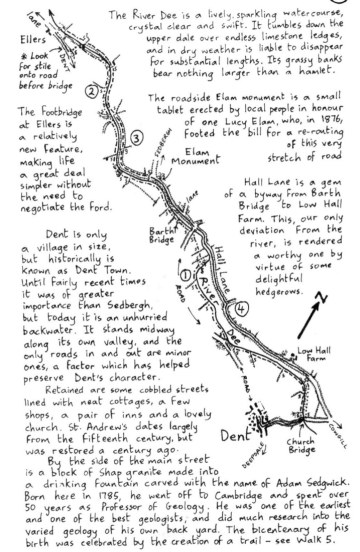

The River Dee is a lively, sparkling watercourse, crystal clear and swift. It tumbles down the upper dale over endless limestone ledges, and in dry weather is liable to disappear for substantial lengths. Its grassy banks bear nothing larger than a hamlet.

Ellers

✳ Look for stile onto road before bridge

The Footbridge at Ellers is a relatively new feature, making life a great deal simpler without the need to negotiate the ford.

The roadside Elam monument is a small tablet erected by local people in honour of one Lucy Elam, who, in 1876, footed the bill for a re-routing of this very stretch of road

Elam Monument

Hall Lane is a gem of a byway from Barth Bridge to Low Hall Farm. This, our only deviation from the river, is rendered a worthy one by virtue of some delightful hedgerows.

Barth Bridge

Dent is only a village in size, but historically is known as Dent Town. Until fairly recent times it was of greater importance than Sedbergh, but today it is an unhurried backwater. It stands midway along its own valley, and the only roads in and out are minor ones, a factor which has helped preserve Dent's character.

Retained are some cobbled streets lined with neat cottages, a few shops, a pair of inns and a lovely church. St. Andrew's dates largely from the fifteenth century, but was restored a century ago.

By the side of the main street is a block of Shap granite made into a drinking fountain carved with the name of Adam Sedgwick. Born here in 1785, he went off to Cambridge and spent over 50 years as Professor of Geology. He was one of the earliest and one of the best geologists, and did much research into the varied geology of his own back yard. The bicentenary of his birth was celebrated by the creation of a trail – see Walk 5.

Low Hall Farm

Dent

Church Bridge

WALK 16

8½ miles

From Austwick

looking north-west

Trow Gill
Clapdale
Norber
Sulber Gate
Norber Boulders
Crummackdale
Austwick Beck Head
Crummack
Austwick

A limestone classic, with the Norber Boulders a famous exception. Generally easy walking, much being along three unsurfaced green lanes.

Park in the village centre, with care as space is limited. ❋ An alternative start-point is Clapham car-park. A glance at the Ordnance map will show how the walk can easily be joined by turning up by the church, under two tunnels to the junction of Thwaite Lane and Long Lane.

THE WALK

From the village centre head east past the inn and left up Townhead Lane. At a crossroads with a rough lane go left along it, but leave almost immediately over a stile on the right to follow a track to a gate. Do not use it, but accompany the wall up to a stile in the corner. Climb the slope behind to a guidepost, to which we shall soon return. For now though, continue up to where a path squeezes between limestone outcrops then fades on the Norber Boulders plateau.

After exploring the attractions return to the post and turn right on a sketchy path above a wall and below Robin Proctor's Scar. Beyond a stile the wall turns sharp left, while our path heads half-left across a large pasture to a stile back onto Thwaite Lane. Turn right along this walled track to a T-junction, then here turn right again along the similarly Roman-like Long Lane. Living up to its name, remain on it to its eventual demise into a green pasture.

Now turn up to the right on a track rising to a stile. Beyond it the track continues more clearly as it wends its way past Long Scar. Avoiding any lesser deviations, a wall-junction at Sulber Gate is eventually reached. Don't use the gate

The top of Norber, looking to Ingleborough

or even the adjacent stile, but opt for the smaller gate in the right-hand wall. A path descends to Thieves Moss: passing between moss and limestone it forks, the cairned right-hand path passing a variety of outcrops and running near the edge of a natural amphitheatre before dropping to Beggar's Stile.

Over the stile a path descends, soon becoming vague but maintaining its direction. An equally sketchy path diverts left to visit Austwick Beck Head, its location being fairly obvious. Back on the original path a stile is soon reached, with Crummack Farm just beyond. Here a gate in the wall in front avoids the farm, and its access road is joined to lead unerringly back to Austwick.

Long Lane runs parallel with Clapdale down to the left, and provides good views of Ingleborough Cave, Trow Gill, and Ingleborough's summit plateau.

* A varied finish can be had by leaving Crummack Lane after it becomes surfaced, at a stile on the left. Drop to a stile by a barn then rise to join a rough lane. Cross straight over, head away with the wall to a stile onto a drive, then through small gates between houses onto Townhead Lane.

Unfortunately there is no public right-of-way onto the very top of Norber (1320'), though one does run to a stile to give access to it!

to/from Clapham (see note on page 58)

As soon as Thwaite Lane is left, the Norber Boulder Field comes into view, with the prominent Robin Proctor's Scar just to the left

Note the footpath sign part-way down the farm road from Crummack, which bears the rarely-seen distance of 1·8 miles!

Robin Proctor's Scar

Norber Boulders

Thwaite Scars

Long Lane

Thwaite Lane

Crummack Lane

Austwick

CLAPHAM   inn

A65   →HELWITH BRIDGE

The Norber Boulders are geological freaks, famous specimens of something the Ice Age brought in. A retreating glacier carried rocks from further up Crummack Dale and deposited them in their present position. What is special is that they are dark Silurian rocks, now atop white Limestone pedestals which have worn more rapidly. They are termed 'erratic' and are also memorable.

Sulber Gate

Long Scar

⑤

Thieves Moss

view ahead to Penyghent

Note the unusual outcrops on the pavement below Sulber Gate.

Beggar's Stile Cairn

Crummack Dale

⑥

Crummack farm appears and Penyghent reappears at this stile

Before taking the stile make the tiny detour to the cairn for a splendid final view of the walk's limestone delights

Austwick Beck Head

Crummack (Farm)

N

⑦

Austwick Beck Head is a fine sight in spate, with the combined waters of several upland becks returning to daylight through a small cave.

Norber is an extensive limestone plateau bedecked with countless cairns on its broad pavements. Morecambe Bay is part of a grand view which also includes a wide panorama of the Bowland fells.

Austwick is a hugely attractive village happily set well off the main A65 road. A small green, a cosy inn, a centuries-old hall and countless tidy cottages combine to create near-perfection.

A Norber erratic boulder

LOG OF THE WALKS

These two pages provide an opportunity to maintain a permanent record of the walks completed

WALK	DATE	TIME Start	Finish	WEATHER	COMMENTS
1					
2					
3					
4					
5					
6					
7					
8					

WALK	DATE	TIME Start	Finish	WEATHER	COMMENTS					
9										
10										
11										
12										
13										
14										
15										
16										

KEY TO THE MAP SYMBOLS

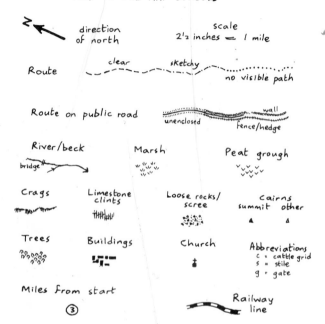

direction of north

scale
2½ inches = 1 mile

Route — clear — sketchy — no visible path

Route on public road — wall — unenclosed — fence/hedge

River/beck — bridge

Marsh

Peat grough

Crags

Limestone clints

Loose rocks/ scree

Cairns
summit   other

Trees

Buildings

Church

Abbreviations
c = cattle grid
s = stile
g = gate

Miles from start
③

Railway line

THE COUNTRY CODE

Respect the life and work of the countryside
Protect wildlife, plants and trees
Keep to public paths across farmland
Safeguard water supplies
Go carefully on country roads
Keep dogs under control
Guard against all risks of fire
Fasten all gates
Leave no litter - take it with you
Make no unnecessary noise
Leave livestock, crops and machinery alone
Use gates and stiles to cross fences, hedges and walls

64